D0561896

THE MISTAKES
OF A *Woman*

Vol 1
A LESSON LEARNED

M. SOSA

Second Printing, 2017
Original print: September 2016

ISBN: 978-0-9951533-3-2

"Love should NEVER feel toxic... that's NOT love."

CONTENTS

DEDICATION

This book is dedicated to *my mother* who is the perfect example of what a mother, a woman, should be. You are the strongest and most humble person I know. Thank you for dedicating your life to making sure we all succeed. You raised a strong and determined daughter. Without you, I would have never achieved everything I have so far in life. I love you.

INTRODUCTION

Everything in this book is a result of *my* past experiences and situations that I've encountered throughout my life. *This book is **not** intended to insult or degrade men or women, in any way.* On the contrary, this book shows *my perspective as a woman,* and common mistakes we sometimes make, that can be avoided.

My goal is for you to relate to at least *one* of the situations and make the necessary changes to better your self-esteem, your relationship, your life. You are in control of your future but in order to want better, you have to do better. I hope my words have an impact on your life, and help you gain confidence back. No more tears, no more sleepless nights, just exhaling... letting all your problems go.

CHAPTER 1
YOUR WORTH

"I'm worth being committed to.
I refuse to let anybody make me feel like I am
less deserving than another. I will no longer
allow anybody to fill my eyes with tears, or
waste my valuable time if they're not willing
to see what a great woman is standing in front
of them. It's not my responsibility to fix
someone's way of thinking, so if I feel like I
deserve better... I'll do better."

I used to be the type of woman that would lower her worth because I wanted a man to want me, to love me. I believed the right approach was to *dumb myself down* so he would appreciate me more. I would tolerate men that *neglected me, cheated on me, broke pieces of my heart*, to take and take and take until I had nothing left to give—until the day came that I no longer wanted to feel that way.

My self-esteem and my self-worth were in big trouble back then. I made excuses and even justified certain situations, that I knew deep within, I shouldn't have. I let these men chip away at my self-esteem as if I didn't matter, and each time I allowed them to do so, I felt as if I didn't deserve any better.

It took me almost two decades to realize how desperate I had become to try to find what love was supposed to feel like. I wanted to know what the meaning of true love was, and like many women, wanted to know what I had to do to get a man to want me *for me*.

I went from one unhealthy relationship to the

next because I just couldn't get it right. I thought I needed a man to find my self-worth. And if one man didn't want me, another one would, or at least that's what I thought things had to be like back then.

I made the same mistakes repeatedly because the main problem weren't always the men I dated. The main problem was ME. Without a doubt, the most important relationship I had to rebuild was with MYSELF.

If others didn't see my worth, it was mainly because I knew I didn't think much of myself either. Don't get it twisted because I took great care of myself. I pampered myself and always looked the part but deep down inside hid a lonely girl that just needed to feel loved by the right man... No, I needed to find my worth and not depend on the love of another to feel complete.

Mistake after mistake, I realized I wasn't alone feeling this way. I witnessed some of my closest friends doing the exact same mistakes I was doing. They would try to hide it but I knew they were in the exact same boat as me.

It became quite fascinating at times watching them give me advice, preaching on how I should do this and do that, yet they wouldn't follow their own advice. "Soooo, I'm supposed to listen and use your advice but you're not using it on yourself? SURE, I'll really listen to you, buddy!" Hence, the reason behind my sarcasm.

These were the same friends that were married or in a long-term relationship, and would allow their husbands/boyfriends to cheat on them repeatedly, keep beating them—and pretend like everything was okay. Ugh, NO! I never took their advice because as much as I knew my issues were bad, theirs were way worse and I couldn't allow myself to take advice from people that weren't doing any better than me.

Throughout the years, I saw all types of women, including myself, lowering their worth to *please* a man that wasn't doing the same in return. No reciprocity at all.

You see, there's the type of woman that would rather go for the *bad boy* that will treat her poorly than the *nerd* that just isn't fit to "sit next to her", or the type of woman that's attracted to a man that's unavailable. They don't care if he's in a relationship or married because if they want you—they'll get you, no matter who they hurt in the process.

There's also the type of woman that keeps up with the nonsense (cheating, lying, abuse, etc.) in hopes that their partner will someday, hopefully, maybe—change.

And then, there's the type of woman that believes that giving her body away is a way to make her partner stay or make them love her, but the reality is, if you're willing to give it away that easily—what makes you think they'll respect and love you after they've gotten in your pants?

It's YOUR body. Respect it.

It's not because you give it up to them that they will want you more, or will want to build a life with you. On the contrary, they might just want to have a fling with you, have sex and leave. That's the reason why many women end up lonely, or end up thinking there are no good men out there, and yet fail to realize that they allowed themselves to be placed in that situation. They allowed themselves to be treated like a piece of meat.

Don't put yourself through that because when you allow yourself to accept less or be treated like you mean nothing, you will keep getting less *each and every single time*.

There are more concrete examples of different types of women that I could give you but I think you get the bigger picture by now.

Do you see yourself in any of these women?

If so, *you are not alone*. There are thousands of women out there like you, my dear. It pains me to say it but you do not appreciate yourself enough to know your worth. You have forgotten what it means to love yourself first.

It's okay—I've been there, and I know what you're going through, but there are different steps you can take to change these habits of *staying with people that do not value you.*

When you allow someone to treat you so disgracefully, you're telling that person they can do whatever they want to your heart and you'll accept it.

You're allowing yourself to stay stuck for years, maybe even decades, with a man that will NEVER *respect you because he knows you'll keep accepting how he's treating you, no matter what he says or does. You'll keep accepting what he's giving you because that's all you believe you deserve.*

You allow men to treat you the way *you perceive yourself,* which means you allow them to get away with murder because you want to make them happy and want to feel accepted instead of realizing that you are the main cause of the problem. The more you keep accepting bullshit, the more you'll keep getting it.

You also fear being alone. Just the thought of being single can be frightening for some of us. Letting that fear win can sometimes keep you in a toxic relationship because you're unsure how you'll feel if you end up alone.

Being single isn't as bad as you think. There is so much growth in knowing you're able to invest quality time in yourself. You learn to not get attached to anyone and learn to take care of your emotional, spiritual and mental well-being instead.

When you start to accept that you are unique and perfect in your own way, you learn to accept yourself for who you are, and not for *who others want you to be*. There's such beauty in loving yourself by learning to love your imperfections, your flaws, and growing from your past mistakes.

Never apologize for being you. You deserve to be treated with the utmost respect. Enough with settling for the worst. Put it out in the universe that you deserve better, or you'll keep receiving garbage. Tell the universe that you are worth being committed to. You are worth meeting someone that will shower you with love. You are worth the effort.

If you keep believing that you don't deserve all of these things, you'll keep falling into a vicious cycle that will just keep repeating itself, until you learn to change.

Do it for yourself and not to appease someone because you expect them to love and want you more. Don't you believe you deserve more than what you're getting?

Think of it this way, if he really cared or loved you, he would want to help you grow into a better version of you. If he's just there watching you drown, why do you keep hoping he'll throw you a life jacket?

You are in charge of who you become, and what you want out of life. Never forget that.

CHAPTER 2
UNDERSTANDING MEN

"Listen and take the time to understand where a man is coming from and you'll conquer his heart."

Be careful how you interpret this chapter and the next few, because in no shape or form am I telling you to pamper your man and become his slave. I am simply giving you concrete examples of mistakes I have made during my past relationships and mistakes many women make in general. Read all the chapters ahead before assuming the worst...

Men and women do not function the same way. Women are far more complex. Men, on the other hand, are known to want to serve and protect us when they are in love, or/and if you're able to inspire them. The moment you can listen, understand and appreciate a man, you will win his heart.

The issue we sometimes have as women is, we don't listen enough to what men are trying to tell us. We don't take the necessary time to understand what is coming out of their mouths. We only hear what we want to hear, and that causes a lot of misunderstandings.

You've got to understand that men do not sugarcoat what they want. *If they want you, they will show it.* If they don't, you will know by their actions. It's not rocket science, but we sometimes tend to complicate things by over thinking every little situation when the truth is staring us right in the face.

Number 1 rule is to never try to pressure a man into commitment or you'll be signing your own heartbreak. Trust me, I've been through this a couple of times and have learned the hard way that *you cannot force anybody to love you.*

A man that wants to be with you will show you immediately or will let you know within the first few months of dating. The more you try to pressure him into a relationship, that he may not be ready for, the bigger chance of him running the opposite direction. Nothing you say or do will change his mind if it's something he isn't ready for.

Are you carefully understanding what you're reading though?

Get it in your head, ladies…
If he isn't showing you the interest that you're expecting, he's just not that into you. You might find it rude or cruel on how I'm telling you this, but I refuse to sugarcoat the truth.

We want men to understand us but we don't always make the same effort to understand what they want from us. We cry out how much we want respect from them but we fail at giving it back to them at times.

Many men will not tell you that they have similar wants that women do… but they do! For example, when you take charge of everything and take full control of every situation without letting him help, you make him feel worthless.

Allow him to take control at times, he doesn't need another ~~mommy~~ mother, he wants a girlfriend… a wife. He doesn't need you to make all the decisions, even if you feel the urge to always do them.

A man also likes to be taken care of, the same way you do. I'm not talking about buying him a $300 pair of Jordans just because he feels he'll look good in them. I'm talking about there being nothing wrong with catering to your man. Take care of him as long as *he is doing the same back to you.*

Compliment a man's achievements, and motivate him into being the best man that he can be. Show him that he is valuable, in other words, *take care of his ego.*

Listen carefully to what he is saying. Pay close attention without disrupting what is coming out of his mouth and you might just end up understanding what a man is all about.

It's not hard if you take the time to simply LISTEN. Don't judge. Don't give your two cents. JUST LISTEN.

CHAPTER 3
CHANGING HIM

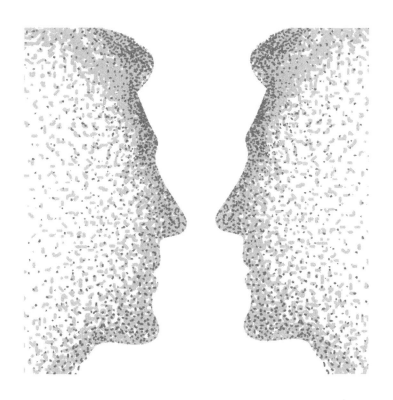

"If he isn't matching your efforts, why do you
persist on trying to change him?
Let him be or let him go."

You want to turn a man off? Try changing him. Try changing the way he thinks.

He is who he is. Take it or leave it. Don't try changing him into being somebody he isn't ready to become. I'm not telling you to waste years of your life waiting around, like a fool, for a man to change his bad habits. I'm saying, trying to force a man to change when he doesn't feel he is ready to, might hurt you in the long run.

I understand you want him to become a better man, or you want him to outgrow his childish ways, but some men aren't ready to take that step yet. Some never will because they don't see an issue with their behavior.

I recall being in a relationship where I tried changing the man I was with. I wanted him to be "this way" and not be "that way". I wanted him to dress classier because his baggy pants weren't cutting it for me.

He would let his beard grow, and it would turn me off. His grooming habits weren't to my liking and no matter how much I tried to change him, he never listened. I would sometimes go as far as insulting his appearance because I figured someday, he would get fed up and would just end up doing things *my way*.

Maybe if I ridiculed the way he dressed, he would end up wearing proper fitting pants. Maybe if I complained enough, he would get the picture and would shave more often. Maybe if I argued with him a little more, he would stop wearing running shoes all the damn time.

That was the mistake right there. I tried to change a man into being my "project" instead of simply accepting him as my man. Trying to make him do things that he wasn't ready for just upset him repeatedly.

Women are caretakers by nature, and we sometimes feel we are doing the right thing by doing it our way, but the reality is, we emasculate a man when we keep shoving things down their throat because they aren't doing things the way we want them to. That's not the way any man should be treated, especially since we wouldn't accept it being done to us.

From experience, you will end up pushing the right man away by trying to change him into someone he isn't. He will one day throw it in your face, like one my exes did.

I remember it like it was yesterday. He said "You wanted me to do this and go there, and that's not who I wanted to be and that's not what I wanted to do. I tried to change to make you happy but I ended up being miserable instead."

I thought I was doing right by him. I thought I was helping him grow but what I was really doing was destroying our relationship, bit by bit. That caused a rift in our relationship, and it eventually ended. That proves to show that things might go downhill if you try to change the simplest thing about him.

He wants to be heard and appreciated for who he is, and insulting him will just make him want you less. It might also make him fall out of love with you altogether. You don't need to criticize him or make him feel stupid to get your point across.

Disrespecting him will only make matters worse. Try saying something nice for a change, something that makes him feel good about himself. You might just end up getting what you want.

How about complimenting how nice his shoes look with his outfit? Or even complimenting the way he's styled his hair today? The smallest gesture can make a huge change in his behavior towards you. He doesn't need you to lie to him, if he doesn't look the part, well don't make a comment at all unless he asks you what you think of his outfit.

If you find ways to compliment his looks and his behavior, you have a far better chance of him changing his attitude towards you.

It's always how you say things and *not demand them* that are the most important. There's a difference when you use a subtler tone than using an aggressive one to express your feelings. Being less aggressive will make him feel more comfortable. Remember, the way you say things can inspire a man to do those changes on his own. Try it, you might just see something good come out of him.

The goal in any relationship shouldn't be to try to change someone. The goal should be to grow together and build a stronger foundation. In instances where you try to change him because you feel that you're doing the right thing, you might end up pushing him away for good.

You might end up causing him more stress than before, and that might be the breaking point where he decides to leave for good. If you don't want him to change you, why would you push him to change for you?

A man that wants to do better and help your relationship grow will make all necessary adjustments at the right time of his life. You will never be able to push him into doing something he doesn't want to do.

When you keep focusing on his failures and flaws, you might end up ignoring your own underlying problems. And as odd as it may seem, when you become obsessed with trying to change him, you might end up realizing that the problem isn't him... it's you. Look closely.

CHAPTER 4
RESPECT HIS PERSONAL SPACE

"Your relationship will flourish when you learn to spend time apart. Growth comes from learning to be alone."

Respecting a man's personal space is very important because sometimes, they just want to be left alone. It's not that they don't want to spend time with you, they simply want to have some alone time without interruptions.

I realized throughout my past relationships that I wanted to be in control of everything. I wanted to know everything. And if I didn't have that, I felt as though something was wrong. The truth was, something was wrong with me and my perception of things. I thought I was trying to protect him, but I wasn't. I was trying to control him. Everywhere he was, I wanted to be.

See, whenever he would get upset at me or simply wanted some alone time, I would berate him with phone calls and texts thinking that would push him to open up.

Quite the contrary to say the least...
I wanted to know what was going on in his head. I believed I could help him and make him feel better, but that simply pushed him further and further away.

It took me years to comprehend that I needed to give a man his personal space whenever he needed it. I didn't have to know everything he was doing or who he was doing it with. If he needed personal time or just needed time to think things through—I had to let him be. In order to understand what he wanted, I had to see things differently by listening to what he needed from me, instead of trying to suffocate him. I didn't need to know his every move.

Ladies, read this carefully and let it soak in.

You don't have to do everything TOGETHER!

If he wants to go hang out with his boys, and doesn't include you, it doesn't mean he doesn't love you. He simply wants some time to be with his friends to hang out, catch up, etc.

Encouraging your partner to do things separately is a healthy way to show your partner you trust him. It also shows him that you are independent enough to be without him and can also have a good time without him being in the picture all the time.

In other words, ladies, get a life (I mean that in the nicest way). Have fun. Enjoy the sun. Go on vacation with your girlfriends. Have a drink, or two. Be productive without him.

Respecting each other's personal space is crucial in every relationship because the day you end up being apart, you'll feel as though something is wrong (when most likely nothing is), and that will drive you insane. You'll end up over thinking and making up situations that aren't really there because you believe you should've been with him instead.

Part of growing together is learning to do things on your own; learning to do things with other people, and knowing when you need to spend time apart... even if it's for a few days. It's healthy.

CHAPTER 5
APPRECIATE WHAT HE DOES

"I'm not the easiest person to love.
I might seem complicated at times, because I
can be annoying and obnoxious. I have a
weird sense of humor that'll make you
question if I'm being serious or whether I'm
being sarcastic. I have faults like everybody
else but one thing you can count on is my
loyalty towards you. I will support you when
everybody else doesn't. I will love you when
it feels like you are alone. I will be by your
side at your worst moments, holding you so
you don't fall. You can count on me to always
be your other half. I won't let you down."

"If only I had done or said certain things differently..." is a line we sometimes use to express our sincerest regrets after a breakup.

One of the many things we overlook is everything he is doing, instead of pointing the finger at all the things he isn't.

I used to never acknowledge all the great things one of my exes would do for me, and would look at all the nitty-gritty things that he wasn't doing instead. I guess a part of me felt that everything was "owed" to me. I felt that if he wasn't doing everything the way I wanted it to, then it just wasn't good enough.

I admit, I was ungrateful and immature with my way of thinking. Instead of appreciating the time he took out of his day to spend quality time with me, I would complain how the laundry wasn't done, the dishes were dirty, or even, him not spending enough time with me (mind you he was working 50+ hours a week). *Selfish much?*

Yes, I was.

I found ways to bitch at the things he wasn't saying or doing. I found all the possible excuses to make him feel as though everything he did wasn't good enough—that was awful of me to put him through that kind of turmoil. He didn't deserve to be treated or to feel that way.

The hardest part was admitting to myself how much he *tried* while I was busy just complaining about the little things he wouldn't do.

If you take the time to appreciate everything your man is doing, he will keep trying to please you. *I'm not saying he will be your servant.* I'm simply saying he will appreciate the way you acknowledge everything he is doing, and will keep on doing it because he wants to make you happy.

A man that truly loves you will do these things for you because he gets pleasure in knowing you are happy with what he is doing for you and how it's making you feel.

So, next time you're about to complain about this and that, think before reacting. It's the smallest gestures that matter most.

-KEYWORDS-
Appreciate,
Acknowledge,
Compliment

CHAPTER 6
NAGGING WON'T MAKE THINGS BETTER

"Respect others the same way you want to be respected. If you don't like something your partner is doing, tell them. They're not psychics and can't always guess what's wrong with you."

Growing up, we're told we're princesses and we'll get married to our future Prince. That perfect man in the movies and fairy tales is nothing but a lie because NO MAN IS PERFECT.

No man will ever give you everything you need and want. Be careful how you interpret this because *I'm not saying* there are no good men out there. I'm simply saying there is no such thing as perfection.

We often create this illusion that the man we end up with is supposed to have it down packed, and when things start to crumble, we start to nag him for the things that are going wrong instead of simply talking things through. A relationship is built on trust and communication. Why is it that we have such a hard time talking to our partner about what is bothering us? What happened to being open and honest with our partners? Instead, we find ourselves nagging them for things that don't matter. We put the wrong attention in the wrong things.

For many years, I found myself breathing down the throats of some of my exes for the pettiest reasons.

Looking back, I sometimes think I got a kick out of doing it. I wanted to see their reaction and I wanted to take out my daily frustrations on them. It was my way of bitching about everything and anything that would come to mind. What I should have done, was *communicate* with them. It would have been easier.

It took me a long time to realize that the only way to make things work in any relationship was to talk about what I was feeling, there and then, not later. It would have avoided us having any type of shouting match or argument.

Nagging and bitching only made things worse. And even though I thought that was the right decision then, I know now that not being able to communicate my frustrations or questions were *my own downfall*.

I learned to be a better woman by opening up and speaking my mind when something was bothering me. Maybe you should try it for a few days... you might just see the same change in yourself. For once, stop nagging and start talking. You'll see a major change in your relationship, and if it doesn't work—well you know it's just not meant to be.

Berating someone is useless, especially when you should be spending your time together making memories. Respecting your partner is the key to a healthy relationship, and it will help nurture it. Your relationship will grow into something you've never experienced before. Something so beautiful... so real.

CHAPTER 7
YOU'RE MOVING TOO FAST

"You cannot force someone to love you.
You cannot force someone to jump into
a relationship with you if they're
not ready to do so."

I believed that love was meant to flourish fast, and moving forward with someone by sleeping with them or spending a lot of time with them was the right approach.

I was dead wrong.

When you spend too much time with someone, at the beginning of any relationship, you fail to see some of the *red flags*. You're more focused on getting to know that person so you avoid paying attention to certain details. It's normal to feel infatuation at first because everything is brand new but that same feeling can get you in deep trouble if you start moving too fast.

Let's keep it real, you don't know the person. You know parts of them that interest you but you don't know all the dirty little secrets hidden in their closet, right? When you become too emotional too fast, you miss out on all the rational things that might be staring you right in the face.

For all you know, he's the opposite of what he portrays. What I'm basically trying to say is that trying to lock someone down too fast will be your downfall because you become oblivious to everything else around you.

Take your time to get to know someone. There's no rush, and there's no need to push someone into a relationship if they're not ready. The worst thing you can do to a man is stress him out or harass him to be in a relationship with you when he's not comfortable or not ready to take that step forward. It's unnecessary pressure.

It feels forced, and that should never be the type of relationship you end up with.

It's better to start off as friends so you get to know the quirky side of one another, than to jump into a relationship and not truly know who you're really with. You don't want to end up sleeping with the enemy because you rushed everything to have it *your way*.

There's nothing wrong in taking it slow. You have all the time in the world to learn new things from one another, like their flaws and their insecurities, but jumping into something you might regret later, can scar you for life, if you're not careful.

Trying to tie a man down at all cost might end up costing you the entire relationship because when a man isn't ready and *he keeps telling you he isn't ready*, and you end up forcing him to jump ship with you, he might end up blaming you for taking things too fast when things start going sour. He also might just end up thinking you're crazy... *either one is a fail*.

Rushing to get married, or to have a baby can also hinder your relationship in the long run because instead of taking your time, you forced something to try to "keep a man", again—WRONG APPROACH.

Both parties involved should be able to make the necessary decisions of wanting a relationship or marriage. It's not always about *your* wants and needs.

CHAPTER 8
IT'S NOT A
RELATIONSHIP

"You've given him months, or maybe even years of your life by being faithful, reliable and supportive. You've dedicated everything to this man, and yet, you can't understand why he isn't able to commit to you... but why would he? If you've given him everything, he's comfortable at this point because he knows you'll keep giving him all of you even if he doesn't give you the commitment you desire. You're ready to blame him for playing with your feelings but the reality is, you should be putting the blame on yourself for accepting everything he's been doing. You're the one that stayed. Nobody forced you. We are sometimes quick to blame the man when we fail to acknowledge that the mistake lies mainly on ourselves for accepting them to treat us that way for so long. If you're not happy with your situation, stop making excuses—leave."

This is one of my favorite chapters because I've done this way too many times to ever make the same mistake again.

Now, I don't know about you but I haven't had many relationships. The few that I've had, have all lasted a long period of time. Have I ever had a booty call? Yes, and I am not ashamed to admit it. Let's face it, we are not all angels.

I could lie and pretend I am perfect and sell you a lie but the truth is, I haven't lived a sacred life. I've been through a lot of life experiences because I was a fool.

When I describe myself as a *fool*, I don't mean I didn't know what I was doing. I'm basically stating that I was young, insecure and naive. I didn't know any better and I had no common sense when it came to men. And only as I got older, did I understand what a relationship was supposed to feel like.

Back then, I thought a man that *wanted* me, should want to take me to the bedroom. If he didn't, it wasn't normal and he wasn't into me. But if he did take me to bed, well it automatically meant that we were getting "closer", which would eventually lead to a "relationship". Right?

WRONG! WRONG! WRONG!

Don't make the same mistakes I once did by believing you must give yourself to a man for him to 'want' you.

Some ~~boys~~ men will lie to get what they want, while others will tell you how it is from the get go, so there is no confusion. And then sometimes, we end up falling for a man that has charm and knows how to sweet talk us by saying everything we want to hear, so he can get into our pants... and then get close to our heart, and BOOM, he's got us trapped.

It's the perfect scenario when a handsome man comes along, sweet talks you, tells you everything you want to hear, from how sexy you look to how he wants to cherish you, wants to one day have a family with you to how he wants to make you his wife someday.

He takes you out, caters to you, courts you and there you go falling for the wrong reasons. Your emotions start to run high because he seems different than the other men you've dated.

There's something about him that just makes him stand out from the rest. So, you end up spending more time with him, slowly falling for him. You see him from time to time, and you believe you're exclusively dating. You *assume* that he wants the same things you want and you'll end up being his woman eventually—time goes by—months, even years—and everything stays the same.

You eventually have the guts to ask him what he wants from you and that's the moment your heart starts shattering to pieces because now that you've invested so much time and effort into him—the words that come out of his mouth are "I just want to be friends... *with benefits*."

Yes, he said it—with benefits (and he didn't stutter so you know it's true.)

Now it gets tricky because confusion starts kicking in. You believed you had something more than just sex all this time. You believed you had something *special* so how could he not want you? I mean, you're the bomb, right? Who wouldn't want to feel privileged to be your man, right?

The situation you're in now is because you went in with your eyes shut and ears closed, instead of asking the right questions from the get go. I learned at a young age that the more I asked questions from the beginning, the less confusing it got afterwards because we both knew what we wanted from one another.

The message I'm trying to relay to you is a simple one—ASK QUESTIONS NOW AND YOU'LL HAVE NO REGRETS LATER.

If you can sleep with someone or give them some of your valuable time, you should be able to open your mouth and ask them from the get go "What do you want from me?" or "What are you looking for?"

NEVER assume you are in a relationship with someone just because you shared a kiss, went on a date or because you've been intimate with them. You are just lying to yourself.

You are creating fairytales in your head of how you expect things to be but not accepting the reality of it all.

A real man, not a childish boy that is into playing foolish games, will tell you the truth. He will not sugarcoat it, and will tell you if he sees a future with you or if he's simply in it for a *good time*.

If he tells you that all he wants is to spend some time with you at 3 a.m.—believe him. He is clearly telling you that he doesn't want anything serious. That doesn't mean he *might* change his mind in the long run. No. He is telling you he wants no girlfriend, no commitment, no strings attached. In other words, he is free to see or sleep with who he wants to and there is nothing you can say about it because he isn't taking what you have seriously. It's just sex to him, nothing more.

My issue with one of my exes was just that. We dated. We broke up. We would start hanging out again, feelings would arise, and then I'd feel heartbroken every single time he would tell me he didn't want anything serious because I **ASSUMED** (keyword ladies... ASSUMED) he wanted a relationship with me, or sometimes even believed we were in one—when we clearly weren't.

We clicked each time we were around one another and that comfort of knowing each other so well is what blinded me. In other words, we clicked but for all the wrong reasons.

Was he an asshole? No. I was foolish, and I believed I was in love with him.

And even though he was my best friend at the time, I knew that the longer he stayed in my life as my *special friend*, the more harm I would keep doing to myself. And I just couldn't keep harming myself that way.

He was my Kryptonite, and probably still is to this day, but I know that we are better off apart than together.

I named this chapter "*It's Not A Relationship*" because the same way I've been through this is the same way many of you have too. We believe we are heading into a relationship, and we make up this beautiful Utopian world in our heads where everything is perfect between the two of us. But when the truth hits us, we become undone and we automatically believe the man is at fault for playing with our heads.

I can't lie but that feeling of rejection really sucks. It feels as though your heart is being torn to pieces and thrown away like garbage, yet we are the ones that accepted to be placed in that situation in the first place.

We cannot blame a man because of our irresponsibility.

Earlier, I mentioned a man will tell you the truth, while a boy will find ways to lie. Know the difference between the two.

A boy will easily play with your emotions and will pretend that he is really into you, will make you feel as though you are his woman, and will play the fields unbeknown to you.

In situations like that, yes, it's normal for you to feel used and sick to your stomach because you got played. I'm referring to situations where a man makes it clear that *he isn't interested* in developing a serious relationship with you, and you end up staying *in hopes* that he will eventually, somehow, change his mind.

That my dear, is you playing with your own emotions. If you choose not to hear what he is saying to you, you cannot get mad at him when he ends up meeting someone else to replace you with.

You cannot get upset if he ends up in a relationship with someone that isn't you because the truth is, he does not owe you anything.

*You are **NOT** in a relationship with him. You are simply a part-time lover, and nothing more.*

I know it's not an easy pill to swallow but once you're able to get this through your head, you'll never make the mistake again of being treated as anybody's booty call or side dish. You will know to accept certain situations for what they are, and leave when the first red flag emerges.

You deserve to be someone's girlfriend/wife, so why settle for anything less than that? Don't you want better for yourself? Then do better by choosing not to place yourself in situations that will bring you heartache and pain.

Stop creating illusions of how things should be and accept them for what they really are now.

CHAPTER 9
YOU COMPLETE YOU

"As I began to love myself, my relationship with everyone changed."

I could have added this chapter with "Your Worth" but I felt it should be set apart to make a point.

I failed at this, many times, because I kept looking for *my father* in the men I dated. My father left when I was barely 7, on Christmas day. Yes, you read that right, on Christmas day. I loved him. He was a great father during those 7 years and even though my mother never spoke bad about him, I always felt like he was a bad influence for the remainder of my life. He haunted me.

My older brothers set great examples for me growing up. They were the only males in my life because my mom never believed in bringing another man into the house, out of respect for her children. She sacrificed her happiness for her children and that is something I will never be able to fully thank her for. My mother provided me with everything I needed and more, and I never missed out on love or affection BUT there was still a part of me that wanted that male figure around.

I wanted a man to complete me because I thought that was the only way I would find happiness. I thought being with a man was the only way I could find true love. Incorrect.

It took me a long time to realize that the only person that could ever truly complete me was ME, and only ME. Everything started and ended with me, and how I felt about myself.

Only I knew how to make myself happy. Only I knew what was right from wrong. Only I knew the type of self-love I needed to feel as though I was "enough".

If you think you need a man to complete you, you are better off single and alone. It might sound harsh but I am being truthful when I say that looking for someone else to make you whole is the biggest mistake you'll ever make. Looking for someone to feel fulfilled will fill the void temporarily, but you will end up in the same place, over and over, until you learn to appreciate spending quality time with yourself. Focus your energy on loving you. Now, keep repeating this to yourself…

morning, noon and night. No matter how you're feeling, and no matter how hard it is, remember:

*"The most important person in your life is **YOU**"*

When you learn to value yourself by not letting anybody make you believe that you need them, you will easily differentiate when the relationship you're working so hard to protect is worth it or not.

You will know what you deserve, and won't allow anybody to give you any less. But the most important lesson of all will be learning to walk away from any relationship that is causing you more harm than good. You won't allow anybody to waste your time, and you won't allow anybody to toy with your emotions for the heck of it. You'll kick them to the curb before that ever happens again.

Now that's *SELF-LOVE*!

CHAPTER 10
GOING BACK TO THE ONE THAT HURT YOU

"Each time you allow the person that broke your heart back into your life, you keep reopening the same old wound. There's a point where you have to say goodbye, good riddance and move on."

When you believe you're in love, you'll do anything to be with that person. You adore them and believe they deserve your time and full attention. You want to protect them, and expect them to reciprocate the same effort you're giving them. Unfortunately, for many of us, that isn't always the case.

I know from past experiences what it feels like to be drawn to someone so deeply you think that each time you allow them back into your life, that maybe this time will be different... but it never is. Things are always the same and never get better. They sometimes end up getting worse.

The mistake I kept making was letting my ex back into my life. Each time we spent a little time together, there was that attraction that lead us back into the bedroom.

And as much as I would like to say it was love—IT WASN'T. It was nothing more than INFATUATION.

Yes, you can lie to yourself all you want but eventually the truth will hit you (and it will hit you real hard), *we confuse lust with love*. We end up going back because we think love has brought us back together again... NOT! It's all in your head.

We make up illusions of what we think our future will be with them. We believe what we want to believe and keep seeing things with eyes shut, instead of opening our eyes to the reality of the situation.

I lied to myself for 8 years. I kept telling myself "This time things will be different." So, each time he would call, I would give in because... *it was HIM*. He knew me better than anyone. He knew me inside out. He knew what made me laugh. He knew what made me mad. He knew what turned me on. He knew what would break my heart, every single time.

The problem was I was always ready to give him all of me whenever 'he wanted me'.

He knew that each time he wanted to come back, I would take him back in a heartbeat. If he called, if he text, if he rang my doorbell, I would always be available... no matter the time of the day.

And even though he didn't know any better, he took things lightly, while I did everything possible to get him to see me differently. I wanted him to see me as his future woman, his future wife but I was kidding myself.

He would make things clear each time he would come back into my life, telling me he didn't want anything serious but I kept taking him back because I thought I could change the way he perceived me.

I thought if I gave him more sex, or changed my bad habits, he would finally see my worth. Wrong once more! He never wanted me *that* way. The only thing he was interested in was my *p*ssy*, and how often he could get it. He wanted his cake and eat it too. Nothing more, nothing less.

Part of me didn't realize until recently why I stopped going back to my ex. I was asking myself the other day why I stopped messaging and calling him, and it hit me.

He had a new girlfriend, and kept comparing me to her. He kept acting as if she was such an angel, and made me sound as if I was the devil. I had made so many mistakes in his eyes, that I just wasn't good enough (he didn't literally say it but I could clearly understand what he meant). *She was better, and I never would be.* I even tried showing him she wasn't such an angel and had another man on the side, but he never believed me.

Me—the only person that had never lied to him.

Me—the only person that ALWAYS had his back.

Me—the only person that only wanted him, and him alone.

The moment he made me sound like a liar; the moment he believed her over me; the moment he replaced me for a cheater, was the moment he lost me *forever*. I realized that he would never see me as the woman who had grown from her mistakes.

He would never see me as the woman who gave him her all and got nothing in return. He would always perceive me as the "*same old Maggie*" from years back... and that's one thing I could no longer tolerate. He would never value me the way I deserved to be valued, and I couldn't accept being treated that way by a narcissist.

We sometimes allow others to lower our worth and we believe that is all we deserve. But that's not how life should be, there's so much of you that deserves to meet someone that is willing to give you the love and attention you deserve. Settling for anything less is pointless.

It's never easy to admit to ourselves that we messed up. We made the wrong choices and because of that, we ended up breaking our own hearts *again*.

The best thing I ever did was learn to love myself enough to never let my ex back into my life. It was hard. It was excruciating not picking up the phone and messaging him, but it was something I had to do or I would stay stuck in the same situation for another 8 years, if not longer.

I knew if I kept calling or answering his messages, or even answering the door—it would just keep going on and on, for as long as I would allow it. The only solution was to stop, ignore and erase everything—and I literally mean EVERYTHING—that would remind me of him. It was the only way to stop thinking of him.

I spent many gruesome nights asking myself the following question, until it finally synced in, and hopefully you can answer it as fast I did too...

"How much more time will you waste taking back someone that will never value and appreciate you?"

Ask yourself that question, and answer it honestly and truthfully. The only person you'll end up lying to is yourself if you don't answer it genuinely.

When a man truly wants to be with you, he will show you with his actions, not his words. If you have to beg for it, he's not the right man for you. You've heard this many times before but for some odd reason, you can't get it in your head. Maybe this time, it will sync in, and you'll actually listen.

If you hesitate, or keep making excuses for his behavior—*you're part of the problem*, and definitely *not part of the solution.*

One of my biggest regrets was going back into the arms of the man that kept breaking my heart. I knew it was wrong, and he was no good for me, but a big part of me wanted him to see how good I was for him.

I wanted what he obviously did not, but I kept looking the other way because I didn't want to face the truth.

Don't make the same mistakes I did. You deserve better than to settle for somebody that doesn't see your worth. You deserve to be showered with loyalty, respect and love… and the right man will give you all of that.

CHAPTER 11
THE SABOTAGE

"The day came when I realized I kept selling myself short. I deserved to be with someone who would treat me with the utmost respect, and deserved to build a relationship with someone that didn't believe a relationship was slowing them down. I required someone that would take a risk at love, and not run away from it. It all boiled down to how much a person was willing to sacrifice to be with me, and if they could make me a priority in their life. That's the type of person I'm determined to end up with—nothing less."

While I believe that there is such a thing as true love out there, I also know that we sometimes sabotage a great future with men who have the potential of being our future companions, future husbands.

You have been hurt a countless number of times, you have been lied to time and time again, you don't trust people like you used to, you won't allow anybody to get too close to you because you fear you'll be let down... I GET IT!

It's never easy to meet someone new. It's sometimes quite frightening because we assume that new person is out to get us, and will eventually just play with our heads, like the others have.

Not all men are the same.

You've got to understand that not all men out there are dogs. There are a lot of good ones out there that have been hurt a countless number of times, just like you and I have. And they also believe there are no good women out there because they've been on the other end of the stick too.

Now, the real question is, how can we give someone new a chance without getting our heart torn into shreds? Unfortunately, there is no way to tell.

You must give love *one more chance*.

You may be telling yourself *"Easier said than done, Ms. Sosa!"*, but I'm dead serious when I say, the only way to find out is to give someone else the benefit of the doubt.

The one thing that's been obvious throughout my life is that once you learn to truly love yourself again, your surroundings will change for the better.

You no longer attract the wrong type of people because you feel real comfortable in your own skin, and you love yourself too much to let anybody undervalue you. By doing so, you attract new people, good people, that are similar to you—whether friends or lovers. And you no longer feel as though you are making a mistake by taking a risk with someone new.

When you're still thinking "He's going to eventually hurt me", you haven't fully healed. You're still building walls up and you're not giving anybody a fair chance to get to know you because you're afraid they'll eventually hurt you the same way your ex did.

You barricade yourself behind those walls because you feel comfortable believing that those walls will protect you against anybody that means you harm. But what you're honestly doing is hiding behind them because you're afraid of being disappointed again.

Stop sabotaging future potentials and start living. It's time to forgive the fools that have done you wrong and it's time to heal, once and for all.

You never know who you're letting go of if you don't take a chance to get to know someone new. They might be completely different than your past relationships, and might show you something to look forward to.

If you keep staying stuck in the past, you will compare all your future relationships with your past—and you'll be stuck there forever.

Over the years, I made so many excuses as to why a beautiful and educated woman as myself, was single. I guess a part of me was embarrassed to admit, I just couldn't meet a *good man*. I also had friends that were in the same boat as me. They would agree with whatever I said, and vice versa, because we thought there were honestly no good men out there. We gave the same excuses all the time from "All men want is sex" to "Nobody finds me attractive" to "I'm good all by myself."

Lie after lie after lie...
These destructive thoughts would jeopardize any hope of finding a good man.

I was covering up my own insecurities. I was scared to get hurt again. I was scared to date again. I was scared to love again. I was scared. Point blank.

I didn't want to find love. I wanted to keep making excuses for myself so I wouldn't have to face meeting someone new. I believed if I kept lying to myself by telling myself that there were *no good men out there* and that *I was better off on my own*, that I would never go through another heartbreak... and that wasn't a way to live. I knew I was trying to avoid the pain, but I had to start facing the fact that love will *sometimes* hurt. It won't always go as planned. Love won't always be easy, and sometimes people will disappoint you in the worst ways. It will also be challenging because it will push you to let go of your past to make way for a better future.

To make a new relationship work, you need to look deep within yourself and face your past wounds head on. You cannot go into a new relationship with the same mentality as before or you'll just end up jeopardizing it.

Another reason people sabotage their relationships is because they like to play make-belief. It's like a safe mode we get into where we create a fantasy of what love is without really feeling it. Everything becomes a routine, and comfort eventually sets in.

Restrictions start to get imposed on one another, and both parties feel limited on what they can and cannot do.

Eventually, there is friction because there is no trust and there is a dependence on knowing what your partner is doing at all times. The destruction ahead is inevitable. You end up becoming your own worst enemy, and end up sabotaging something that could have potentially worked.

When you can accept that you are a loving, vulnerable individual—you allow staying open to the idea of finding real love. Keep in mind, there is no such thing as a *perfect relationship*, so why keep stressing yourself out on trying to find one that is?

The longer you keep searching for perfection, the harder you'll find it to meet someone that meets your "perfect" criteria.

- Allow yourself to meet someone new.
- Allow yourself to be vulnerable once more.
- Allow yourself the freedom to express your needs and wants.

If you believe you deserve someone good in your life, they will eventually find you. But if you keep believing that you are not good enough, you will keep attracting the wrong type of people that will keep taking from you.

How you perceive yourself will help you catch the right fish. And for all you know, you've probably thrown the right fish back into the sea thinking he was the same as the last. If you don't give love one more chance, you will never know when the right one comes along...

CHAPTER 12
LET GO.
BREATHE.

"Someday, you will come to the realization that all the hurt and pain weren't for nothing. The heartbreaks you've endured and wrong people you met throughout your life won't be in vain, because eventually you will experience the right type of love with the right person. No more games, no more playing with your emotions, no more trust issues because that person will show you what true love is all about. They won't sell you a dream and change within a few months because they will be entirely devoted to you, and you alone. Yes, there is such a person out there for you. Did you really think that out of 7 billion people in the world, none would be compatible to you?"

Letting go is one of the worst feelings you'll ever have to experience. It's an excruciating pain, that you think will last forever. At that moment in time, your heart hurts, your body aches, and you feel like you want to die.

"You feel like you're hyperventilating because you can't breathe without them"

You feel like you can't function without that person in your life because you've grown so accustomed to them. Everywhere you look, all you can think of is *him*. Everywhere you turn, you think you see *him*. Every man that passes by you smells of *his cologne*.

I remember my pillow, drenched in tears, because I couldn't understand what went wrong in my relationship. I would toss and turn in my bed, feeling like nobody cared about how I felt. I had friends and family tell me that it would be okay and all I could say to myself was "No, it won't be because HE won't be around."

All you can think about are the plans you made for the future, and how you both should've had *forever*. You're supposed to be happy. You're not supposed to feel sad, but all you can do now is think of what could have been and how things should have turned out.

Every minute of the day, your only focus remains on him and what you could've done to change things around. *What if you had done this? What if you had done that?* Your mind keeps taking you back to past moments and you can't help but wonder, what you could have said to make things right.

The first few days are the hardest because you go through different emotions. You become angry, then sad, then happy and back to sobbing over a container of ice cream. You barely sleep because of the restless nights over thinking. Every situation goes through your mind, and it feels as though time is passing by too slowly. A big part of you feels like you will never be happy again because *he was the one*. You feel like you'll never want to love anybody else either because you're loyal to him, even though he broke your heart.

You're so in denial, that all your energy is wasted on going back and forth in your mind, wondering if everything happening to you is true. Is he really gone? Is he out of your life for good? How can he be okay without you by his side? Doesn't he love you? Doesn't he care how you feel?

A million questions flood your mind, stopping you from living. You keep hoping and praying that something will change. He will wake up and realize that he messed up, and will make things better—but that never happens. You begin contemplating going out but if you do, you might miss his phone call. That part of you just wants to keep waiting around for him, waiting for him to smarten up. You basically depend solely on what his next move might be towards you.

Most of the time, he never ends up calling because he wants nothing to do with you. If he wanted to call, he would have.

The other part of you is telling you to get back up and stand strong. That inner voice is telling you to fight for yourself because nobody will do it for you. I mean, you can't just sit around moping all day, thinking of what could have been and just let your mind keep going in circles. You should go out and do something, but what?

This gets interesting because I know how this plays off for the most part. You end up going out with some friends and figure "Why not take some selfies and load them onto Facebook and Instagram?" Maybe that will show him that you're having a marvellous time without him and he will want to come back to you. Or how about you start flirting online with one of his friends so he gets jealous, and that gives him a reason to message you. *Some kind of communication is better than no communication at all, right?*

See, all these tactics are the wrong way to approach a break up.

Believe me when I say, when he breaks up with you, he's already busy living his life and not worrying about what you're feeling. I know it hurts to read this but many men that end a relationship, do it for a reason. What happens to you afterwards is none of their business because they're done with you and in their mind, they owe you nothing. You can cry, you can yell all you want but nothing will change his mind if he's unhappy.

You can be in a new relationship and flaunt it over the Internet, and that still won't change the way he sees you. The crazier you get, the more attention you'll put on him—the longer he'll think you still want him, and that will make you look like the 'desperate ex' that can't get over him.

What I'm desperately trying to show you here is that we, as women, have a heart that will give, give and give until we have nothing left.

When a man leaves us, we feel as though our whole world is ending but the reality is— YOU WILL SURVIVE.

Breakups happen every day, and although they hurt, things will eventually get better. I have done it several times and I've picked myself back up stronger and better, each time. It will tear you up inside for days, weeks, months or even years but one thing I can tell you is *things will get better if you let them.*

The longer you keep obsessing why things ended, why you're not longer together, why he replaced you with someone else... the longer it will take for you to heal.

I'm definitely not telling you to suck it up and get over it. I would be heartless if I said it like that but I am telling you to focus your energy on all the good things in your life that don't include him.

Spend time with family. Join the gym. Go out with friends. Live your life, and don't stop living because he's not worried about how you're feeling.

And it's okay to be vulnerable because nobody expects you to be bulletproof. So, if you end up crying while you're out, CRY, CRY, and CRY some more. Nothing feels better than letting all your emotions out. Sometimes, that's all we really need. You just want to know someone can relate to your pain, and can listen to your heartache. You feel comfort in knowing that everything will be okay because if they survived, *so will you*.

From my past experiences, I can truly tell you that the only thing that helps with letting go is *TIME*.

People will tell you to meet someone new, or join an online dating site but time is the only thing that will help you ease your pain.

Slowly but surely, you will stop caring what he's up to or who he's with because you'll be too busy worrying about your goals and your growth. You'll be so busy living your life, fulfilling your dreams and reaching new heights, that anything that reminds you of him will be a thing of the past.

I've been through a few heartbreaks that have taken me years to get over but in the end, I try to always remember the good times and let go of the bad ones.

We're all different, so no matter how long it takes you to get over someone, just make sure you're not losing sleep over someone that isn't losing any sleep over you. Remember, there are more than 7 billion people in the world, you're not the only one going through a heartbreak. You're not the only one that's crying. You're not alone.

Let go and breathe again. It's time for you to exhale... a new beginning is waiting.

To be continued...

Writer's Passage

My Mistakes Turned Into My Lessons

My mistakes are what made me into the woman I am today. I am a strong, independent, mature woman that knows her worth and I am no longer weak at the thought of him. I no longer fear being loved by the right man either.

At a young age, I believed being in total *control* all the time was the right approach in a relationship. Never letting my guard down and watching a man's every move was the way to catch a good guy. All that ever did was bring me misery, and I wasted years of my life. That wasn't a relationship. It felt like kindergarten spying, watching every move my man would do.

As I got older, I realized that everything I went through taught me a valuable lesson that help me build stronger and meaningful relationships with the right people. The type of relationships I've always dreamed of... the husband potential type. The great friends type.

I knew what it finally felt like to be surrounded by people that genuinely cared for me, instead of people that only cared about what they could get out of me.

I also learned that sometimes people grow apart, and there's nothing wrong with that. It could be you, the same way it could be your partner. You might still love each other, but sometimes people need time and space to figure things out.

As a loving partner, you must love the person enough to give them the necessary space they need. It doesn't mean you will end up back together, but it also doesn't mean you won't.

If you want to stay stuck in the same hole, in the same toxic relationship, you will. Only YOU can make the necessary changes to better yourself. It always starts with you, remember that. If you want to do better, you will.

"Accept the fact that not everything is meant to be. The fear of moving on is holding you back from getting what you deserve, so you settle for simply being comfortable. Don't let that fear win."

Your Notes

Your Notes

Instagram
www.instagram.com/sweetzthoughts

Facebook
www.facebook.com/sweetzthoughts

The Mistakes Of A Woman
Volume 1: A Lesson Learned - 2016

Made in the USA
Middletown, DE
16 May 2017